Christian CHALLENGE

Collected Poems

VOLUME III

Bill Granse

Greenville MI 2016

authorHOUSE®

AuthorHouse™
1663 Liberty Drive
Bloomington, IN 47403
www.authorhouse.com
Phone: 1 (800) 839-8640

Published by AuthorHouse   11/11/2016

ISBN: 978-1-5246-4945-6 (sc)
ISBN: 978-1-5246-4944-9 (e)

Print information available on the last page.

Any people depicted in stock imagery provided by Thinkstock are models, and such images are being used for illustrative purposes only. Certain stock imagery © Thinkstock.

This book is printed on acid-free paper.

FOREWORD

"Christian Challenge" is the third book of poetry authored by my brother, Bill Granse. In the last several years, Bill has concentrated on communicating his thoughts about God and Christianity in his poetry. My brother's, strong Christian faith is evident throughout his poems and has sustained him through the many difficult parts of his life.

This book would not exist without the kindness and sincerity of the of the congregation of the "First Congregational Church of Sheridan Michigan," a small agricultural community in Central Michigan. For several years my brother attended church there as it was near the foster home where he resided. Thru the years, the Church accepted and printed many of his poems in their monthly newsletters.

In the summer of 2015 when this book was envisioned, the Church kindly supplied me with back copies of their newsletters from 2008 to the present. The retrieval of these poems made this volume possible. In a few cases spiritual poems are presented which were not in the Church newsletters.

The poems have been arranged from works describing individuals that despair and have been rejected by society, and then proceeds to the author's challenges to live life according to Christian principles. The volume concludes with poems best described as praise to God and Christ.

It is refreshing and uplifting for me to state that my brother has done a superb job adhering to the principles about which he writes. It is a personal challenge for me to try to emulate him in this, and a pleasure to have assisted in editing this book.

Richard Granse

INTRODUCTION

It is an honor to be, once more, completing a book of poetry that is published by Author House. As far as my previous two books were concerned, I appreciate the cooperation I received from Author House and from my brother, Richard P. Granse.

The third book is somewhat different from the others. In this book, I include primarily poems written for the First Congregational Church in Sheridan, Michigan. My view of Christianity is found in this book, as well as commentaries on other religions. I am not trying to give the readers a moral lecture. This is simply my view of certain aspects of life, and problems people have to solve in this world, as well as in life in the "next world." The Christian's view of life after death, as well as his relationship with God is included in this book.

This book is dedicated to Sanderson M. Smith, Jack Petzoldt, and the late Scott Chisholm.

Bill Granse

Contents

The Card Players

You know them: the card players in bars, college dorms, and
psychiatric wards.
They lose money at cards instead of giving it to the Lord.

Sometimes they win, when they lose they take it hard;
And they can't get to Heaven by playing cards!

Christ said, "In my father's house you do not gamble."
He drove the money lenders out, by means of an example.

Wars and rumors of wars come and go, but the card players stay
the same.
They'll find on judgment day that they played a losing game.

To their surprise, when it comes time to leave this land,
The card players will find that they held a losing hand.

Sometimes they win, when they lose they take it hard;
And they can't get to heaven by playing cards.

A Phone Call To Heaven

Did you ever call a guy who said, "I can't be your friend!?"
That's his way of bringing the relationship to an end.
But you don't have to start to cry or to call nine-eleven.
Just ask Jesus when you make a call to Heaven!

Some people will reject you. They're conceited and they're cold.
They'll say you're too young for them or that you're too old.
But be sure you don't think that's it the end.
Just make a call to Jesus, and he'll be glad to be your friend!

Some people will ridicule you. They'll look at you and laugh.
But you don't have to hit them or bother to laugh back.
You don't have to start to cry or to call nine-eleven.
Just ask for Jesus when you make a call to Heaven!

George Green

George Green's enemies thought he was a pest,
Because he prayed to God and he did his best.

People borrowed his money and never paid him back.
They said George's mind was on the wrong track.

But George plodded along doing his little bit of Good,
Helping people out whenever he could.

George just lived his life day by day,
And never got in anyone's way.

His enemies thought George was really odd,
Because he read the Bible and he believed in God.

But when George died, he went to Heaven up high,
And his enemies went to another bye and bye!

In The Eyes Of Christ

Some people may be hurt by what others may say,
But Jesus doesn't hurt people that way.

If you're a mental patient or a homosexual, you may be rejected.
In fact, you may be ostracized if you're even suspected.

The way people treat you may not be very nice,
But everyone is equal in the eyes of Christ!

Christ will forgive you if your cocktail party is too long,
Or if you happen to do something wrong.

Even if you're a thief or shoplifter,
Christ will forgive you, mister!

Sister, you may think that you've got a raw deal,
But Christ loves you, no matter how you feel.

The way people treat you may not be very nice,
But everyone is equal in the eyes of Christ!

Ronny's Life

Ronny's friends wouldn't leave him alone.
They teased him and insulted him right in his own home.

They were his friends when they wanted to borrow a buck,
But they avoided Ronny when he was down on his luck.

They made Ronny buy them drinks when he was in a bar,
Then they laughed at him and said he wouldn't get very far.

Ronny was afraid it would always be that way;
Then suddenly God chose to take him away.

Now that's Ronny's in heaven, things aren't like they were before.
He's with God now, and people can't insult him anymore!

When You Get To Heaven

Did anyone who owed you money ever write you a bad check?
Or did someone deal you a card from the bottom of the deck?

But those things won't happen in your home beyond the blue,
Because when you get to Heaven, everything will be good and true.

Some people will reject you, and that really hurts.
There will always be some people who treat you like dirt.

But when you get to Heaven, nobody will play this game;
Because in God's eyes everybody is the same.

In this world, people murder and rob banks.
They will take all you have without giving any thanks.

But these things won't happen in your home beyond the blue,
Because when you get to Heaven everything will be good and true!

Joe Finally Came Home

Joe Thompson lost one apartment after another and kept bumming around.
Everybody said that he'd never settle down.

When he was young his dad kicked him out of the family home,
And after that all he did was roam.

He lost job after job and didn't have any friends.
He just wished that his life would come to an end.

Then one day, Just as his whole world was falling,
Joe Thompson heard Jesus calling!

After that, Jesus talked to him every day,
And when Joe died, he went to Heaven to stay!

Happiness At Last

Joe wasn't a very good man, but he wasn't really bad,
And suddenly he lost everything he had.

He didn't have any money or friends,
But he didn't realize that God was with him to the end!

Joe's health was poor and he didn't have medical care.
He wanted to protest, but he didn't dare.

He was bitter and lonely and he showed it.
He had the Grace of God, but he didn't know it.

Then without warning there came a wind from the east.
And suddenly, somehow, Joe found peace.

Now Joe is a happy man, which isn't so odd:
Because now Joe knows that he has found God!

He's Standing By

George went to a spiritualist meeting.
Joe saw a lawyer because his wife was cheating.
But before you search for help far and wide,
Remember God is on your side!

To see an attorney or a psychiatrist is fine.
You pay your money, and they sell their time.
But if you are ever on the verge of despair,
Remember that God is always there.

Lot's of people will give you advice.
They may do it just to be nice.
But before you search for help far and wide,
Remember that God is standing by your side!

Peace

Lucky was so nervous that he could hardly think.
The bartender laughed and said, "Have another drink"

When Lucky left the bar, He thought he was over the hill.
He thought he would feel better if he took all the pills!

Then a friend of his gave him some advice, that Lucky thought was odd.
His friend thought that Lucky should get in touch with God.

Then, out of the blue, Lucky felt free from his worries and fears.
When he started to pray, he calmed down for the first time in years.

He had been trapped by his own thoughts, but suddenly he got his release.
Because when Lucky turned to God, he finally found peace!

The Shores Of Lake St. Claire

I remember the day on Lake St. Claire,
　　Spring was in the air,
And God was there,
　　On the rocky shores of Lake St. Claire.

I remember the day I met you there,
On the rocky shores of Lake St. Claire.

I said, "marry me," and you said, "I will;"
　　But God sent me a warning that I'd better beware,
On the rocky shores of Lake St. Claire.

You said that you'd see me there the next day,
But I waited for you then, and you'd gone away!

Now, I'm back by Lake St. Claire,
　　Spring is in the air,
And God is there,
　　On the rocky shores of Lake St. Claire!

We Are Not Alone

My high school English teacher said he
    Saw about four thousand kids come and go.
How many more, he did not know.

We may lose a friend or acquaintance
    And take it hard;
But no matter who we lose, we've still got God!

We have our good days, and our bad.
We may inherit some money,
    Or lose our mother or dad.

Someone said that life is like acting on a stage.
We come closer to God, every day that we turn a page.

We may lose a friend or an acquaintance
    And take it hard;
But no matter who we lose, we've still got God!

Where To Turn

Some people, when they are depressed,
    Turn to drugs and liquor.
But that will only depress them quicker.
When things are going wrong and life is hard,
The one you should turn to is God.

Some people think they have got life all figured out.
But they do not really know what life is all about.
They say they do not need a psychiatrist or
    They do not need the Bible.
But they will find that God is always available.

It is easy to be angry or to be a quitter.
And it is easy to turn to drugs and liquor.
But when things go wrong and life is hard,
The one thing you should turn to is God.

A Sin Against God

Illegal activities like money laundering or stealing a car,
Are also a sin against God.

A person may hit someone, and do some things that are unheard,
He may even commit a murder.

He may know what's right and do otherwise,
But God is watching from on high!

A crook may think he can fight the law and win,
But someone up there knows that he has sinned!

An alcoholic may get help from "AA,"
And God can help him fight his problem all the way.

If you lead an evil life, you're not going up any higher,
And some people believe you're going down in hell's fire!

Anyway, for some people the next world will be hard,
Because hell is separation from God!

The opportunity is there for every man,
To be part of God's glorious plan.

Another Supreme Court

In this life,
If you have a complaint,
You hire an attorney,
And the court sets a date.

But someday, you will stand or fall,
When you go before the highest court of all.

When you leave this world,
God will show the way,
When you present yourself to him,
On Judgment Day.

If you have led a Christian life,
Heaven will be your fate;
But if not,
It will be too late.

Someday, you will stand or fall,
When you go before the highest court of all!

Don't Wait Too Long

Some people don't realize how much they've lost
When they wait until they're dying to creep to the cross.

Whether your're young or you're turning old and gray,
You should relate to God every day!

Often people don't know what religion is all about.
They wait until they're in trouble to have God bail them out.

But whether you're in trouble or whether you are not,
You should always relate to God.

It's too late to shoot for heaven when you're dead,
Because then you'll probably go to hell instead.
Whether you're young or you're turning old and gray,
You should relate to God every day!

Free Salvation

You can get saved any time you chose.
God will be with you,
Whether you're mentally ill,
Or have the Asian Flu.

If you're in jail,
Or there is trouble at home;
God is with you,
You are not alone.

If you don't believe there is a God,
Or you wonder why,
You better change your mind,
Before you die.

If you decide to accept God today,
You have your salvation,
And nobody can take it away!

If you have hard luck, but survive,
You have Him to thank.
God has so much love,
You can put it in the bank.

You can decide to let things go,
When you are over the hill,
Or you can be saved,
You have free will.

If you decide to accept God today,
You have your salvation,
And nobody can take it away!

Get Involved

Some people don't give of themselves; they just let the world revolve.
They spend their lives doing nothing, they don't want to get involved.

If your friend has a problem, do you help get the problem solved?
Or do you avoid him because you just don't want to get involved?

With the bad economy, there's a lot going on at home,
Do you help the situation, or do you just want to be left alone?

What do you think of the President's health care bill?
Are you helping to get it passed, or are you content to let it be killed?

Now I've got a question; try to answer it somehow:
If Jesus Christ didn't get involved, where would we be now??

God Is Everywhere

An atheist will say there is no God,
But that's neither here nor there.
Of course, God is up in heaven,
But he can be with you anywhere.

Some people will call on Him
When they fall flat on their face.
God wants them to pick themselves up,
And get back in the race.

God really has no beginning and no end.
Regardless of your age, He can be your friend.

Don't be like the devil's angels in Heaven,
Who were cast out of there.
As Garth Brooks says, "God will help you,
By not answering some prayers."

You can't be as good as God,
No matter what some people might say;
But if you elect to serve Him,
You will be rewarded on Judgment Day!

You can be God's servant,
Whether you succeed or fail.
God won't forget you,
Even if the court puts you in jail!

People who think their life has been hard,
Will be surprised when they learn
That they are saved in the eyes of God.

You may lose some friends,
Your relationships will be severed;
But you must realize this life
Won't last forever.

The Bible says to forgive your enemies
Seventy times seven;
But this will be in the past
When you spend eternity with God in Heaven!

God's Plan

I met a man who thinks he's superior, I don't know why;
But he'll find that everyone's equal when he dies.

Some people strive for success, walking over everyone in their way;
But they'll learn their lessons on the Judgment Day.

You may have a big bank account and a lot of land,
But his won't help if you don't follow God's plan!

You may have an attractive house and a fancy car,
But these things alone won't get you very far.

You should stay in touch with God every day.
And don't let the devil stand in your way.

You may have a big bank account and a lot of land,
But this won't help you if you don't follow God's plan!

On Time For Judgment Day

Joe was a guy who was always late.
When he was supposed to meet a friend,
He was late for their date.

After work he liked to roam.
While his wife waited for him;
He was late getting home!

He was no angel,
He went his own way;
But he will have to be on time,
To face God on Judgment Day!

Once he was late to testify in court,
Antagonizing the prosecutor and the jury;
Because again, Joe was in no hurry!

Joe was never on time,
No matter what people might say,
But he'll have to be on time,
To face God on Judgment Day!

Recovery

All my life I've been in trouble,
Losing jobs and in trouble with the law.
I started drinking
Which didn't help at all.

Everytime I tried to solve my problems,
I fell flat on my face:
But when I finally stopped bar-hopping,
Everything else fell into place!

When I started to write I was advised
I would never get published because I was incapable.
And like a lot of people,
I accepted that label.

Some of my friends suggested I cut down on my drinking,
And get a part-time job.
To my own surprise I did this
With the help of God!

My educational background and the church,
Didn't give me a hand.
So I fight my drinking
With the help of God I understand.

I didn't know how I could stay off the bottle for long,
When I first joined "AA."
But then I learned to stop drinking,
Just for today.

It was a long pull,
But I realized the people who said I could stay sober
Were not deceiving me.
When I told my bar- room
Friends I had stopped drinking,
They just didn't believe me.

The "AA" treatment helped me a lot,
But some people kept drinking which was silly.
In any kind of treatment
The clients have to have some nobility.

I wanted to change,
And though some individuals still thought I would fail;
I no longer accepted their label.

It doesn't matter whether an alcoholic
Is in Grand Central Station or his own back yard,
He can stop drinking with the help of God!

Returning To Christ

For a long time in our society,
The psychiatrist was God.
But the pendulum is turning,
Now that times are getting hard.

With terrorism and other problems,
That throw politicians for a loss;
We are coming back to the one
Who died on the cross!

Some people say we are in
An Anti-Christian situation;
But if you accept Christ as your Savior,
You've got your salvation!

There are a lot of issues,
Staring us in the face;
But if the American people give themselves to Christ,
Everything else will fall into place.

Lots of peoples are upset
About gay marriages and the Affirmative Action ban,
But the one upstairs knows
What is best for every man.

Some people think we are in
An Anti-Christian situation,
But if you accept Christ as your Savior,
You've got your salvation!

The Last Hour

Good people shouldn't be afraid to die,
Because they'll be up with God in the sky.

However, when it comes to a Christian's time to go,
He may admit that he really doesn't know.

He may be staring into darkness and feel odd.
He may wonder, "Where is God?"

If, however, he feels ashamed.
God doesn't think he should be blamed.

When a Christian says he's taking death hard,
He actually means he doesn't intend to be separated from his God.

The Christian should let God lead him away from the grave;
If he does this, he surely will be saved.

Like Billy Graham and others who did right,
A good man will have eternal life.

The Most Important Vote Of All

The 2008 election is out of the way,
And the Republicans and Democrats have had their say.
McCain and Obama were ready to answer their country's call.
But did you cast the most important vote of all?

If you're depressed and life is hard,
Be sure to go to the polls and vote for God!

Most people forget their problems and celebrate this time of year.
And they know that God is near.

Even if our dreams have been shattered,
At Christmas time our problems don't' matter.
It's too bad life can't be like this all the way,
But Christmas comes another day.

If you're sad after Christmas has come and gone,
Vote for God and you can't go wrong.
If you're depressed and life is hard,
Be sure to go to the polls and vote for God!

To Find God

In my hometown, I'll never forget,
The old man who said, "Have you found him yet?"

Well, when God comes around,
I hope I am somewhere I can be found.

Everyone has to find God in his own way,
Whether it takes 10 years or one day.

You don't have to look for God in outer space,
Just so we make the world a better place.

My 20 year old friend, Michael enjoys when he can do good.
He accomplishes more than most older people would.

He was doing missionary work in Guatemala at last report,
Instead of depending on his family for support.

If you are kind to your friends, and forgive enemies seventy times seven,
You will meet God in heaven!

You don't have to look for God in outer space,
Just try to make this world a better place!

To Find The Way

You may be a sinner and still get saved today.
You have to find God in your own way.

Whether you're an executive who drives a fancy car,
Or a drifter hanging around a bar,
You can always receive God's grace.
It can happen any time or any place.

It may take ten years, or it may take one day:
You have to find God in your own way.

It doesn't matter who you are,
Or whether you search near or far.
It doesn't matter what other people do or say;
You'll find God in your own way!

The Christian Solution

Some people have problems, and can't come to any conclusion;
But Christians find God as their solution.

No matter what the atheists may say,
Most people believe that God will show them the way.

Some wait until tragedy hits them hard,
Then they decide to turn to God.

Christians believe that God will help them do what's right,
Not get revenge or start a fight.

Lots of people want to get to Heaven any way they can,
But Christians believe that God came down to the world as a man.

Even if their life has been hard,
They turn to the three-personed God.

If they follow the Son of God without any doubt or confusion,
Eternal life is this world's conclusion!

The Gifts From Heaven

Why are people allowed to lie and steal and kill?
The answer is that God gave man free will.

Although some people try really hard,
There's no way they can second guess God!

Some people do evil things right along,
And then blame God when things go wrong.
But God gave me a conscience and common sense, too.
These are things that we already knew.

We get many gifts from Heaven above.
But most of all, God gives man his love!

For Better of Worse

One of my friends is going to say, "I do."
I hope God watches over her and her husband too.

You can never predict what will happen in life.
You can only try to do what is right.

Whether you marry a millionaire, or you marry some clod,
You should be aware of the presence of God.

Not all marriages are happy, of course.
Today, one out of every two ends in divorce.

But I think my friends will make it because they are going to try hard.
And they will be aware of the presence of God!

God Is Greater

A friend of mine says, "There is no heaven and no hell!"
When I contradict him he says, "How can you tell?"
But to be honest only God knows
Because God, of course, is greater than us both.

Some people steal and kill and never go to jail,
But someday they will have to answer to God without fail.
The police can't catch them, that's the way it looks,
But God is greater than both the cops and the crooks.

Some people lead lives of depression and despair.
Some try to lead good lives and some don't care.
But they are never out of God's sight,
And someday God will make all things right!

God Will Take Care

Some people say, "Love God until it hurts."
While others just preach "do good works."
But only God knows what's right and true,
And He will always take care of you.

The evangelist says, "to Heaven we go."
While the atheist loudly hollers, "No!"
The agnostic says, "I don't know."
But the Bible says to forgive them seventy time seven,
And only God knows who will go to Heaven.

There are many theories that people advance.
Some say, "Heaven is sure," and others say, "we don't have a chance."

But God watches over everyone, not just a few..
And He will always watch over you!

God's Love

One thing I think is extremely odd,
Is how men sometimes think they are God.
Some of these men are so reprehensible,
That they make life miserable for Blacks and homosexuals!

God loves everyone, that's nothing new.
He loves all people including different people too.
If things are going well, You've got God to thank.
He's got so much love you could put it in the bank!

God loves everyone including Blacks and Jews.
If you think you're better than others, you're really confused.

If things are going well, you've got God to thank.
He's got so much love, you could put it in the bank!

My Best Friend

My friend is always honest and fair,
Because he worships the One up there.

He never looks for trouble, because he knows that isn't right,
But he will never run away from a fight.

He tries to be everyone's friend, even if that seems odd,
Because first and foremost, he is a man of God.

He will help you out if you are in trouble,
Because he realizes that anybody can make a mistake and stumble.

Sometimes you are right, and sometimes you are wrong,
But he will be your friend all along.

He will help you get to Heaven instead of under the sod,
Because my friend is a man of God!

My Great Friend

I recently made a new friend,
Who is my inspiration:
Even though he doesn't have
Much formal education.

He demonstrates his love for God,
By doing things for others.
Though I am a stranger, and no relation;
He always treats me like his brothers.

My friend has a job,
And does volunteer work for the church.
If you need to find a man of God,
You could go to him first.

His good deeds are many,
Although he is still a young man.
I wish I could be more like him,
Though I don't think I ever can.

Whatever he does, he works hard.
And most important, he works for God!

To Neil

Neil Kosht is with God now, not underground.
While he was living he was a nice guy to have around.

His happiness must have been heaven sent,
He wasn't rich or famous, but he was content.

He grabbed my hand before he died.
I guess that was his way of saying good-bye.

Neil made a lot of friends,
He had a good life until it came to an end.

He wasn't hot tempered and he wasn't a fighter,
He wasn't at all like this writer.

Neil Kosht is with God, not underground.
While he was living, he was a nice guy to have around.

My memory of Neil will never grow dim;
It was a privilege to have known him!

To Scott

My friend, Scott, wrote a great book, but for him it wasn't hard.
Scott succeeded in everything because he loved his God.

Scott had a lot published, but he wanted no glory or fame,
Because everything he did, he always praised God's name!

Yes, Scott loved to write, but he loved one thing more.
Because more than all his literary success, Scott loved his Lord.

He wanted to write another book, but time ran out somehow.
But Scott is very happy because he is with God in heaven right now!

To Timothy, My Friend

Timothy is my best friend,
And he will follow Christ right to the end.

He knows why Christ died on the cross,
And I know he will never get lost.

Timothy helps his friends whenever he can,
Which is the quality of a real man.

He firmly believes in God,
When things are going well or life is hard.

To people he knows, Timothy is nice;
And most important he follows Christ!

My Friend in Heaven

During the holidays, until New Years Day,
People will celebrate Christmas in their own way.

Some people will hit the bottle hard,
But my friend will be up there in Heaven with God!

Even though he left this world in October,
My friend's celebration isn't over.

Lots of people will look for a bar,
But people like my friend will be happy where they are.

When it's my time I'll try not to be late,
Because I don't want to make my friend wait.

He left this world so suddenly, I couldn't say good bye.
But I knew he would be happy up there so I didn't cry.

During the holidays some people will hit the bottle hard,
But my friend will be up there with God!

The One Up In The Sky

In this world, we should give our
Friendships the best shot;
But most important,
Is our relationship with God.

Some people worry about this,
When they slip and stumble.
They only call on God
When they are in trouble.

But different people believe
In different ways.
There is a Higher Power
Watching over us each day.

To fully understand God
Is difficult indeed:
But he sees that I have
Everything I need.

There is no God,
The Atheists insist,
But there is all kinds of evidence
That He exists!

Christians believe in the Three Personed God,
And Muslims think there is One;
But God is looking out for the world,
When all is said and done.

The global warming trend and the ISIS people
Won't destroy us all,
Because someone up there
Is on the ball.

We should give relationships
In this world our best shot,
But most important,
Is our relationship with God!

Why Do They Fight

Some people say, and I think they're right,
That the different religions shouldn't fight.

Sometimes they criticize and they hit each other hard,
But they should remember that we're all children of God!

Today Christianity is under attack,
And some of the Christians are fighting back.

Some people may think Christianity is pretty odd,
But when all is said and done, we all worship God.

From the time we're born until we're under the sod,
No matter who we are, we're all children of God!

God Knows

Now, this may seem to be very odd,
But some people think they can put one over on God.
But God knows whether you are doing wrong or right,
And He will watch over you all of your life.

Some people live a life of luxury and ease.
They think they can sin whenever they please.
But whether your life is easy or hard,
One thing for sure, you are not fooling God.

You should have a relationship with God all the time,
Whether you are a good person or whether you are out of line.

You can go to church every Sunday or spend the day in a bar,
God will always know where you are.

You should try to do good while you live,
But whatever you do God will forgive!

When He Returns

We know that Jesus will come again
The only trouble is we do not know when.
The non-believer says, "You'll have to show me"
The agnostic says, "Wait and see."

We do not have to worry about what non-believers say,
Because Jesus made a promise that He would show us the way.

Whether He comes in one hundred years,
Or whether He comes back today,
When you die and they put you under the sod,
Jesus will lead you to heaven and to God.

Forgiveness

What does Christianity have that other religions lack?
Some say when you sin you can't take it back.
But no matter what you've done or how you live,
Jesus will always forgive.

"I've done nothing wrong," some people say.
Others say that we sin every day.
But true Christians are not at a loss,
Because Jesus paid for their sins on the cross.

Today Christianity is under attack.
But Christians have something that other religions lack.
No matter what you've done or how you live,
Jesus will always forgive.

The Necessity Of God

Billions of people need God.
To figure out the reason isn't hard.

I believe in the three-personed God,
With Christ as the Son.
Muslims believe their God
Is the only one.

Christians believe, to accept Christ as your Savior,
Is to have your salvation.
Yet this isn't accepted
By the "third world nations."

Some people think there is simply a force
That set everything in motion.
Although I am a Congregationalist,
I can understand this notion.

Of course, there are Atheists,
Who contend there is not God at all.
They cling to their ideas,
Whether they stand of fall.

Although I am a Christian,
And prefer my own church;
I realize that some people feel,
We get Heaven and Hell here on earth.

When I talk about God,
Some individuals ask, "why?"
But I plan to join Christ
Up in the sky!

Part Of The Action

In many respects,
Life is like a race.
But we are all God's children,
Whether we win, or settle for second place.

There's nothing to be ashamed of,
If you lose the race.
But nothing gained
Is the disgrace.

There must be a God,
Who sets things for us in motion;
Whether we live in Michigan
Or across the ocean.

If you end last in the race,
And wonder why.
You can always ask the referee,
Up in the sky.

If we want to please God,
And gain satisfaction,
We must know His plan,
And be part of the action.

Printed in the United States
By Bookmasters